T0078137

GOD *and* ME

RUTH

WESTBOW
PRESS®
A DIVISION OF THOMAS NELSON
& ZONDERVAN

WestBow Press books may be ordered through booksellers or by contacting:

WestBow Press
A Division of Thomas Nelson & Zondervan
1663 Liberty Drive
Bloomington, IN 47403
www.westbowpress.com
1 (866) 928-1240

ISBN: 978-1-5127-7511-2 (sc)
ISBN: 978-1-5127-7510-5 (e)

Library of Congress Control Number: 2017901832

Print information available on the last page.

WestBow Press rev. date: 02/03/2017

Come, and let us return unto the Lord: for he hath torn, and he will heal us; he hath smitten, and he will bind us up.

After two days will he revive us; in the third day he will raise us up, and we shall live in his sight.

Then shall we know, if we follow on to know the lord; his going forth is prepared as the morning; and he shall come unto us as the rain, as the latter and former rain unto the Earth. (Hosea 6:1–3)

This verse tells us how God lets us go though things, but in the end, he picks us up, kisses our booboos, and makes us stronger than before. This is telling us that life is not easy, and we will fall, and he wants us to know he is there to catch us.

My grandchildren, I'm here to tell you that your lives matters so much to me, and I was even thinking of you when I watched my own babies sleep in their beds. And I loved you before they were old enough to have you. But the love I have for you is nothing compared to the love God has for you.

ACKNOWLEDGMENTS

I want to thank my cousin Michelle who had a hand in my reaching out to people with my stories. And thank you to my husband, Jeremy, who stood behind me while I wrote this book.

CHAPTER 1

THE YOUNGER ME

$\mathscr{I}$'m writing so that you can know that God is real. I pray that by the time you finish this book, you can say with all your heart, "Thank you, Jesus." This book was never meant for anyone but my grandchildren. I don't need my name in lights; I know he knows my name, and he knows your name as well. He knows your every thought before you even think it. He is there when you think you need him the most, and he is there when you don't think you need him at all. By the time you get through reading this book, you will have found out that much of my life revolved around needing God's approval—until finding out that I already had his love.

When I was fifteen, I tried smoking and got sick. I already knew it was bad for me, so thank God he let me get sick, because I never picked up that bad habit.

I did not do the things the other kids my age were doing, so they called me names and picked on me. Maybe that's why I liked to stay away from people. I wasn't popular in school—unless you wanted to point out Miss Goody Two-Shoes. That was in 1985, a long time ago, but I still don't care for name-calling. We lived in Camden, which is a small town in South Carolina. See, you don't have to live in a big city to feel out of place.

I started standing up for myself, which meant I became very familiar with the office—which is not a good thing. But soon people learned I was not going to be picked on. Because of that, I stayed off to myself most of the time. I heard God calling me, but I was young and didn't know how to answer him. My mama took us to church every Sunday, so I went to my preacher and told him that God was calling me. He told me I was too young for God to use me. That tore my heart apart. I cried because, to me, that was the worst thing in the world he could have said. I didn't tell my mama about our talk. I was ashamed for going to him at all. But I'm here to tell you that he was wrong—you are never too young for God to use you. And if a pastor won't help you, then you are talking to the wrong one. Find another pastor!

From that point on, I started going behind my mama and daddy's back and sneaking out at night. I would go to places I hadn't been before. I called a bar one time, pretending to be eighteen, and talked a man into coming and getting me, my sister, and a friend of ours. We went to his house, where I tried drinking. And I even had sex—all because one person told me God didn't want me. When you go out like that, bad things can happen. That night, I got more than I planned for, and the next morning, I felt God's sorrow for me. I realized I just didn't fit in being bad. I was down and heavyhearted and lost with the thought that God didn't want me, so why try to be good? Well, it didn't take me long to figure out I didn't want to do that kind of stuff. And the people I was calling my friends weren't really friends if they were pulling me into that kind of life. You do stupid things when you feel like you have nothing left to lose and when you think your life doesn't matter anyway. God knows we all make mistakes and do things out of pain. So God got me out of doing the wrong things, and then I was back to trying to do the right thing—but doing the right thing isn't always easy. This world wants you torn up and torn down. My kids paid the price for my wrongdoings because I saw how easy it was to sneak out of the house. So as an adult, I never slept well. When they moved at all during the night, I was up!

Someone I knew had seen how down I was and set me up with an older guy. He was twenty-two years old. He saw me at my friend's house and wanted to meet me. People called him Monk. He was not too good with girls. His girlfriend of three years had just left him for another guy. So I understood his pain of not fitting in and not being wanted. This was what I had been praying for, a guy who would love me. He even started going to church with us. But I lied to my mama and daddy about his age. This was just before I turned sixteen, and I had been praying for someone to love. I had been asking God why I couldn't find someone to love me. It seemed like my sister had all the boyfriends and all the friends—and I had none. I had no one, so I talked to the only one I did have—and that was God. So when I met this older guy, he knew I loved going to church. And I thought we had something no one else had. I had never been in love before, and I had never had anyone act like they cared for me like he did. We would talk on the phone for an hour at a time. He would come over just to see me after he got off work. It was as if he wanted to spend every moment he could with me, and I had never had that. I know you're thinking, *You were only fifteen.* But you see, I had no friends and no one to talk to; I felt alone in this world, and it's a big place to be alone in. When you're lost and feel alone, it doesn't take much to get you sidetracked. At fifteen, I wanted love, but who didn't? We dated for three months, and he asked me to marry him. I said yes. We were supposed to go to the fair, but instead we when to the house of one of his friends. This was 1985. His friend pretended to be a pastor and pretended to marry us. That was the only way he could get me to do anything with him, because I wanted to wait till we were married.

We did end up getting married for real but only after I got pregnant. After we were married and I was about seven months pregnant, that's when the cheating started. When we would go from my mama's to his, he would always take a road that was out of the way. I was with his sister one day, and she went down this road, and I found out why he would go down this road. It was because the girl he was supposed to marry lived on that road. His sister wanted me to know where his true love lived. This girl had been sending me messages that she could take him back if she wanted to. Just being mean, see she was watching over him, and he was watching over her. I know losing someone is hard. Letting go sometimes is harder. But know that sometimes people are only in our lives for a season. Only God knows how long they will be there. So there I was, crying and seven months pregnant. I went back to the girl's house and called her out. We talked for about thirty minutes, and I didn't get any more messages from her after that. I let her know who I was and that even though we had only been together for a short time, I would not give him up without a fight—and a fight wasn't what she wanted. I wasn't mean to her, and she was nice to me, and we came to an understanding that she would not send me messages anymore, and I wouldn't go back to her house.

Then a few weeks later, I got sick. I had appendicitis. I was home alone when they found me. I was on the floor and had to have emergency surgery. I was seven months pregnant with my oldest son, Steven. By the grace of God, I still carried him full term. He weighed 9 pounds, 13.5 ounces.

My ex-mother-in-law, when I was pregnant with my daughter, asked me if I had a name picked out for a girl yet. I said, "No, not yet." She gave me the name of the girl's house I went to and said, "If you name her that, I will still have a Tina in my family." Some people are mean for no reason at all. They had a bad childhood, a bad stepparent, a bad parent, or no parents. There are no excuses for being mean. The meaner you are, the harder life will be, but on the other hand, you can be the best person you can be, and life is still hard. The only thing that makes this life better is Jesus. It doesn't matter what anyone tells you. Jesus is the best thing in your life. When you want him as much as he wants you, your life will tell a story, a God story.

We had three kids together—Steven, Jeanette, and Jacob. He was not a good man to me and not a good father. See, he liked to play mind games. When I was pregnant all three times, he would put cigarette butts in my drink while I wasn't looking or tell me I was nothing and that nobody would ever want me. No matter what

I did, it was never good enough. God was with me all of the time. And God had a plan; I just had to wait.

It seemed like I had been fighting for my children forever. My first husband wanted me to get an abortion with both my sons, and then I found myself fighting for them after they got here. I have been on the defense now for thirty years. Everything about my kids was a fight, including getting them Christmas and birthday presents. My first husband didn't want kids. He let me know the only reason he married me was because I was pregnant. So let me tell you, being pregnant is not a reason to get married, but I did. And when I had them, I loved them more than anything in this world. My little treasures that I had to keep safe from the world because, to me, everyone wanted to hurt them. I always made sure they had what they needed, and by the grace of God, I was able to do it.

CHAPTER 2

MARRIED LIFE

*M*y oldest son was a little over a year old, and my only daughter was about four months old. My first husband and I got into a heated argument about him calling 900 numbers. The phone bill came in, and he had run it up to almost three hundred dollars. With two small babies, when they went to bed, so did I. He would stay up at night even if he had to work the next day. We could barely pay our bills, and now we were not going to be able to pay this phone bill. Back then, 900 numbers were call-girl numbers, so to me, he was cheating. He didn't agree that just talking to them was wrong. I told him if he called them again, I would take the kids and leave him. That's when he started hitting me. He was about 265 pounds, and I was about 169. He started slapping me around and threw me to the floor, pulled me up (yes, I was fighting back), and pushed me against the wall with his fist balled up ready to hit me. I told him to go ahead and do it. He threw me on the floor again and yelled, "What are you going to do? Call your daddy?" I told him right back that I never had my daddy fight my battles.

I picked up my crying babies and went to my bedroom to put them out of harm's way. See, he didn't know that when we moved to the country, my daddy gave me a gun, because sometimes we were alone until ten at night. I went to my bedroom and loaded my gun that he didn't know I had. I waited for him to come to the bedroom. When he walked into the room about twenty minutes later, he thought he was going to come in find me crying. Instead, I shoved the barrel of the gun into his chest and told him that as much as he thought I loved him, I loved me more—and I pulled the trigger. By the grace of God, the gun jammed. He could not believe I just tried to shoot him. He immediately took the gun from me and took to the back door to show me there were no bullets in it. He pulled the trigger, and the gun fired. He shot all three bullets I had.

See, my daddy has this saying: if you can't hit it within three shots, then run. God was there with me, and he stopped that gun from firing—because where I aimed, there would have been no coming back. But after that night, it took him a long time before he had nerve enough to hit me again. Besides, God still had plans for him. One of those plans was getting me my youngest son, Jacob.

My daddy likes to say he had a hand in that. So, my son, you now know why you act so much like Grandpa! God had a plan for you. See, I was on birth control and got sick, so Daddy gave me some antibiotics that knocked out the birth control. And I got pregnant. Now I have you, and no matter how bad you think you have messed up, you can never mess up so badly that I would turn my back on you—because I too have messed up, and God never turned his back on me. God sometimes does things in a funny order. And you don't know what the outcome will be, so remember to always trust him, and you won't go wrong. And above all, know that you are never too far that you can't call him—he will always be there.

In my first marriage, there was cheating. My husband did it more than one time. After three years, I wanted him to hurt like he hurt me. So I did what he was doing to pay him back for the pain he had caused me. The thing was he didn't care, and over time, my love turned to hate. He was abusive, mentally and physically. He was so mean to me that I would lie in bed and try to figure a way out. It seemed hopeless. See, abused women don't know how to get out without someone showing them the way. When he stopped being able to hurt me, he turned to the only thing in this world that mattered to me, my kids. He started being abusive to them. That is when I got two jobs. I had to get away before one of us ended up dead, and I knew I had it in me to do it. So I prayed to God and told him, "I can't do this without you, and I know you have better for me than this." I became very bitter toward my first husband.

CHAPTER 3

MEDICAL EMERGENCIES

*W*hile pregnant with my youngest son, my oldest son fell and cut his arm from his wrist to his elbow. He was just three years old. He went running across the yard to kiss my daddy good-bye—he was leaving for work—and he fell on a piece of glass. It took ten stitches inside and thirteen outside. But it got infected overnight. His fever shot up to 104 degrees, so the doctor put him in the hospital. He was in there for four days and getting worse. It was February 14, 1990.

Two doctors came in and told me they wanted to cut his arm off to save his life. They needed me to sign the papers they held in their hands. I signed them and told the doctors that they were not cutting off his arm. They scheduled it for seven o'clock the next morning. It was nine o'clock in the evening when they left the room, and I called my mama, hoping she was home from church. I told her what I had just done, so she went back to the church. She and the people still there prayed to God to save his arm. That night, I went to sleep asking God over and over again to please not take my son's arm. Well, let's rewind. After I signed the papers, they had to x-ray his arm so they would know where to cut. After the X-ray, one of the doctors decided to do one more culture, which is when they run a Q-tip through the cut. Now, let's fast forward to one o'clock in the morning. I was woken up by one of the doctors, and he had an X-ray in his hand. It showed that there was a piece of glass left in my son's arm. It showed up on the X-ray. On the last culture they did after the X-ray, they discovered that the Q-tip got the glass out. He woke me up at one in the morning to tell me that they canceled the surgery. They were going to give him twenty-four hours to show improvement. That was all God; his power and mercy saved my son's arm. When the sunlight came through the window the next morning, his fever and the swelling were gone—and you couldn't tell he was sick at all. And he still has both of his arms to this day. He is almost thirty years old, and he knows that it was God who let him keep his arm. They were going to have to take it off at the shoulder, but when God stepped in, his power took over and healed my son. See, he had been on antibiotics for four days and was no better than when he was admitted. Sometimes we go though things just as a reminder that all we have to do is call on God's name, and he will fix it—but only if we believe.

As it got closer for me to have my youngest son, I still had not picked out a name. God talks to me or sends angels to tell me things, as you will read in this book. A month before my youngest son was born, God sent an angel to tell me something in a dream. The angel was like a shadow coming to me. He told me in the dream that the baby would have a rough start, but he would make it. I told my mama about the dream, and she said it was just a bad dream, not to worry. I knew it was more, and I did worry.

On August 13, 1990, my youngest son was born. They had to do CPR on him three times in the delivery room.

When the doctor could finely sew me back up, he asked what my son's name was. A whisper in my ear said told me his name, so I replied, "His name is Jacob."

The doctor said, "A fighter name for a fighter." I asked if he would be okay. The doctor replied, "He had a rough start, but he's going to be fine." So you see, God was there the whole time, and he knew what I was about to face, and he let me know he was there with me before I even got there. And then, by giving me his name, he showed me he was by my side when I felt alone.

I was lying there helplessly and watching them work on my newborn baby to save his life. Then God reminded me of the dream and how he had already warned me about my son having a rough start. Then the doctor repeated what was said in my dream. He watches over us even when we can't see clearly.

My youngest son was just over a year old. He was playing with his brother and sister in another room of the house. My oldest son ran into the living room where I was and told me that his brother was choking. When I got to where he was, he couldn't breathe. I tried to get what he was choking on out, but I couldn't get to it. I got all of them in the car as fast as I could. My first husband was driving. As we got to the hospital, there was blood running down the side of his face; he was gone. I didn't know at the time what he was choking on.

A man met me at the car and asked, "What happened?"

I replied, "He was choking." Then the man took him from me and ran into the hospital. I was right behind him. He went in a room and shut the door, shouting for me to get out, and all I could do was cry. Crying out, I said, "God, please don't take him from me!" I said this over and over.

It seemed like hours, but it was only minutes. I finally heard him crying. That was the sweetest sound I have ever heard.

It was a screw that almost took my child's life. Not only had I watched him lose his life at birth, but I held him in my arms as he slipped away. God gave him back to me again.

All right, I told you about the boys. Now let me tell you about my baby girl and how God healed her legs. Their biological daddy would make fun of people. That is not nice thing to do, and you should not do it. When I was pregnant with her, he made fun of this man walking down the road that had one leg shorter than the other. When she was born, her legs would not stay in the sockets like they were supposed to. The doctor said, "She is going to have to wear braces on her legs." He wasn't sure if she would be able to walk. During every doctor visit I took her to, the leg bone that went into the hip was out of place, and they would have to pop it back in. She was about nine months old when they started talking about braces on her legs. I thought about what my husband had done. So I prayed and told God, "I had nothing to do with that." Then I asked him, "Take this from her."

The doctor was amazed when she didn't have to have braces on her legs and the bones started staying where they were supposed to. Yes, she walked at the age of thirteen months old. So you see, God healed her legs. She started walking just a little after turning a year old. God is faithful to those who believe in him, and no, you don't just call on him in the valleys; God wants to hear from you when you are on the mountaintop as well.

CHAPTER 4

A NEW BEGINNING

So I am not perfect. I have stumbled, and I have done things that I'm not proud of. Every person does things that they are not proud of at one time or another. See, there are tests we go through in our lives, and if we pass it the first time, we won't have to go through that one again. Just know that, like a video game, for every level you pass, the next one is harder. If you fail, you will be tested on those grounds again.

It is part of life. You must learn from your mistakes or you will do them again. Just know that God wants you to pass the tests, and he walks with you, right or wrong. He is there. And Jesus went to the cross so that your wrongs would be made right. So make sure you learn something from your mistakes. Make sure that when you get tested again, you will pass.

No, I didn't always pass the first time; I too have let God down. I pray that you do a better job than I did. I hope this helps you.

Life is hard with someone that only loves themselves. In a marriage, you have to love each other and let Jesus control the marriage. See, I loved him, my first husband, but there was no room for me or our kids in his life, because he came first and only thought of him. I worked to pay bills and get what we needed. He worked but only for himself; he only wanted to do what he wanted with his money, and that wasn't paying bills or buying diapers or clothes. He didn't even want to buy Christmas presents, so I would buy what I could though the year without his help, but I was blessed because I had Jesus, God, and my three babies. No one could take any of them from me. And over time, I realized that what I thought love was wasn't love at all. And that life wasn't what I was meant for; love is not supposed to make you feel alone and unwanted.

I stayed in that marriage for almost nine years. I left and went back four or five times in that time frame. Like any other woman, I didn't want to take my kids from their daddy. So I would go back to him. He would say, "Things have changed; I'm not that man anymore." But the first time we fussed, he would always say, "The kids don't belong to me anyway. And I never wanted kids."

I didn't help because I would say, "No, they don't, but they have the same father." Just in case you don't know what I mean, I'm talking about God. He is father to us all. When everyone else has given up on you and has written you off, he is still there with his hands out to you.

So after almost nine years, I left for good. I was working two jobs to pay for my trailer and my van. Then I found out he was stealing money from my mama and daddy. When I found out, that was it. I couldn't stay any longer. The difference this time was I said, "God, I believe you have something better for me than this."

We had been apart about five months when a comet passed through the sky. It was in November 1996. My kids showed it to me, and I said, "God, they say wish upon a star, and you grant wishes that are bigger than a star, so here I go. I wish you would send me a man that would treat my kids like his own, who doesn't mind paying bills, and who loves me the way I should be loved." I did date but no one I thought was good enough to bring around my small children. And it was very little dating. Remember, I was working two jobs, and their father didn't give me any money to help. His child support was set at ninety dollars a week, and to avoid paying child support, he ran to Kentucky. It was fine with me; he never helped anyway.

My kids did not know I was dating. I only went out when it was late. Sometimes I wouldn't get off until 10:00 p.m. I didn't want to wake them if they had school the next morning. So they would stay the night at my mama's house, but I was there when it was time to wake them up for school the next morning.

My kids are my world, and guys don't understand a woman putting her kids before him. I came to found out there are not very many women who do that. When a single mama is working two jobs, it is hard to get time with her kids. So to take time from them to spend with a man just wasn't happening. Then after praying for a good man, God heard my cry. That's when I met my husband now. He was funny and made me smile and made me feel like a woman again.

When we met is a funny story. This shows you that God likes to make us laugh. He started working at one of my jobs at one of the biggest retail department stores around. I was sitting on the floor putting out some new Easter dresses when he came around the corner and almost fell on top of me. He was not watching where he was going. He said, "I'm sorry. My name is Jeremy."

Because I had been hurt badly in my marriage, I was scared of what I felt for him. I had never felt this way, not even with my first husband. So I wasn't sure what this was. He was very handsome and very sweet, which I was not accustomed to. He told me he was looking for someone to settle down with. I told him I had three kids and wasn't looking for anyone even though with him I was feeling a love I had never felt before. I even told him, "Jeremy, you need to fine someone that can give you kids because I can't have any more."

We ended up dating; he met my kids. When they met, it was like we had been a family from the beginning, but first I had to make sure they got along with no problems. We moved in together. He wanted to get married the first day we met. But it took two years before I trusted him enough to make that step. The kids had never had someone who, when mama said no, would overrule and tell me I was being too hard, so they loved him right away.

Well, where we worked, you weren't allowed to date a coworker. So he ended up losing his job. The next job he got was a gift from

God. It paid more money, but the hours were hard because we only had one car and sometimes we both had to be at work at the same time. But I only worked six hours, where he would work twelve hours. So I would drop him off at 3:30 p.m. and then go to work. I would have to get up the next morning at 3:30 a.m. and go pick him up. On those nights, my kids stayed with my mama and daddy.

Now, we are on a night that I had to get up at 3:30 a.m. to pick him up at work. At this time, I was still working two jobs, so I was not getting a lot of sleep. Anyway, I had gotten home around 11:30 p.m., had a bath, and got into bed about midnight. So I was sleeping when my bedroom filled with the most beautiful light. This is very hard to describe. With this light, there was a voice that called my name and said, "For your own safety, you must get up and go pick up your Jeremy." I looked at the clock. It said 2:27 a.m., so I said, "I still have an hour to sleep." The voice repeated what it said and added, "I am going to touch you on your forehead, and you will wake up, and you must leave *now*," and when it did, I woke up. It was dark in my room, and I looked at the clock. It said 2:27 a.m. I did just what the light said to do; I didn't even change out of my pajamas. I went to his work, parked in the parking lot, locked the doors, and went back to sleep.

That morning, he got off work early. He thought he would have to wait on me, so he was surprised when he saw our van in the parking lot. He asked why I was there and still in my pajamas. So I told him what I saw in the dream, and he asked, "What would have happened if you had not left?"

I said, "I don't know, but I wasn't going to wait around to find out." When we got back home, it was the time I would have been leaving to go pick him up. There sitting on our front door steps was a black panther. He didn't run away. He walked away! At one point, he stopped, looked back at us, and his eyes were red, not yellow like you see when your lights hit an animal's eyes. This just isn't something you see in South Carolina.

We would not get out of the van for about fifteen minutes. And Jeremy was worried the panther had not gone far, so he told me to stay in the van until he could get the door open. I never saw it again. I know he was there to kill me, but my God would not let it happen. See, he still has work for me to do before I can go home. When God has your back, no devil can hurt you. See, there are angels assigned to us to help keep us from harm that has not been Okayed by God. Job in the Bible shows us that everything done to us has to go through God first. The angels help us to find our way to God.

CHAPTER 5

MY IN VITRO EXPERIENCE

*A*fter that, God opened a door for me to get a better job so I wouldn't have to work so much. This job gave me more time with my kids and was better paying. It was an outside job, which I love doing. It was working for the state. I hope you learn two things from me. First and most important, love God and Jesus with all your heart, not your mouth. It makes a difference. Second, always be the best person you can be. When you have to make a decision on something, let it be one you can face yourself in the mirror with.

This new job also gave us insurance to go to the doctor for us to have a baby together. See, my husband didn't have any kids of his own, and I could not have any more without a doctor's help. When we went, we found out he could not have any on his own. He would need help. The only thing left for us was in vitro. This is not as easy as you think; there are lots of shots and pills you have to take to build your body up to a point where your body thinks it is pregnant—in hope that you at least have one baby out of three. Well we had seven embryos. The night before going to the doctor to get them put in place, I had a dream that the nurse came in and called me back. And when I went through the door, she said the doctor needed to talk to me. She took me to a room. The doctor came in and told me three of my babies had died the night before, and I only had four left, and she wanted to put them all in place.

I woke up in tears. I told my mama about the dream on the way to the doctor's office the next day. When we got there, my dream became a reality, so I took that as a sign to put them all in place. I told the doctor about my dream, but I didn't listen to the doctor, and I returned to work to soon. I was supposed to be out for two weeks, but I didn't have enough leave time, so I had to return to work after a week. I ended up miscarrying our babies at four weeks. I know they are with Jesus, and they know I love them very much. There are all kinds of pain in this world; I wish I could save you from this one. It took me a long time to see a baby and not cry. God held me through this time.

There are things God does that we don't understand. But you have to know he does what is best for you no matter how badly it hurts. Sometimes that's what it takes to get our attention. Then there are times when we are doing well, and he lets us know that he sees us.

CHAPTER 6

PROTECTION AND PROVISION

*G*od protects us even when we don't know we need it. There was this time I was cooking, and the grease got too hot. I didn't realize it. I put whatever it was I was frying into the grease, and it boiled over, and fire covered me. My husband and the kids were standing there, and I did not get burned. We got the saltbox and poured it on the fire. When we got the fire put out on the stove, I heard, "Look up." And on the ceiling there was the shape of wings outlined in black. The reason I didn't get burned was an angel was there with me and blocked the fire from me, but I felt the heat anyway.

Now, when you think you are alone and you have no one to talk to, when you think there is no one who cares about your deepest hurt or your most painful memory, you are wrong. God cares about it all. In the Bible, he says he knows the number of hairs on your head. Now that is love beyond any other that you can find in this world. And he gave us things as well for being good.

One time while I was working, I had a dream, and in that dream I was told, "For all the good deeds you have done, there is a hundred dollars lying in your path today." I got up the next morning and told my husband about it. I said, "Now that was a dream—a wishful dream." I went to work. At the time, there was a lady I worked with who was loud and cursed a lot. I didn't like to work close to her. Anyway, that day we had to pick up trash on Highway 1 in Logoff in front of a tire shop. I was picking up when she crossed the road and started picking up beside me.

Well one of the guys was going on down the road, and I got in the truck and left too. She wanted me to stay with her, but I didn't. In ten more steps was my hundred-dollar bill, and she got it instead of me. That's what happens when you don't lesson to God. So when God sends an angel to talk to you, listen. They're bringing you a message from Jesus. But when you're bullheaded, you will miss out on what God has for you.

That reminds me of another time God gave me money. One of my kids was sick, and I had to take them to the doctor. I didn't have the money to pay the copayment. I was going to get off at noon that day, and my mama and daddy were going to loan it to me. Well, I was cutting grass at a stop sign, and there was a twenty-dollar bill. My copayment was fifteen dollars. God once again was there and gave me the money, so for once I didn't have to borrow it.

See, I don't believe in that "being at the right place at the right time." Because God already knows your every step before you take it; he knows where you're going to be. So that you know without a doubt, God puts things that you need where you will be the one to find them.

There was one time I needed to get milk, and I thought about it at a stoplight. Then I said, "I don't have the money." I saw a something roll toward the truck and stop. It looked like money. So I jumped out of the truck as the light turned green. I reached down and picked it up and was getting back in my truck when people started blowing their horns. That's when I saw it was what I needed to get milk—a five-dollar bill.

So when you find money on the ground, always say, "Thank you, Jesus," no matter how small or big it is. It is all a gift from him. Life is hard even with God by your side; there is no way you would want to go through this world without him. The job I had working outside was one I loved. And I worked with a group of people that treated me like a person. That meant a lot to me. When you work somewhere, always give your best to your boss. Out on the road, most of the time I didn't have any money. I would buy a twenty-five-cent cake just so I could use the bathroom at the stores. Sometimes I didn't even have that. But God did, and on those days, I would find twenty-five cents or a dollar to buy a cake. The guys would tease me; they would say that I was just tight with my money. The truth was I made sure my kids' lunch money was paid and bills were paid, I gave what I could to church, and I made sure my husband had what he needed. And if there was nothing left, it was okay. I was thankful to have a better job. On those days when I had no money, before lunch I would pray that we would be close to the shop, or have to go to the shop so I could go to the bathroom. Then I would find what God had for me. Many times, he gave me money. I can go on and on about what God has done for me. God has always been there to save me. I'm so glad I have God in my live.

I had a lot of close calls with cars and trucks on the road in the five years I worked there. On June 21, 2001, I developed a higher relationship with God. On that day, it started out just like any other. The sun was shining, not a cloud in the sky.

CHAPTER 7

A TERRIBLE ACCIDENT

I was cutting grass on Highway 34, and I was on a tractor. It was a straightaway, and when I looked back, I saw an 18-wheeler. I was past my fear of them. This one was going to be different. He didn't see me until it was too late. He tried to stop; he slid about two hundred feet before hitting me. By the time he stopped, he was all the way up on my mower, just before hitting the cab of the tractor I was driving. My tractor jackknifed before we stopped. The seat had a short back on it. Where the top of the seat was, it broke my back. The truck had four indentions in the bumper, and no one could figure out where they came from. But when I saw the pictures, it looked like fingers to me, so I like to say God put his hand down and said, "That is far enough." The doctors tried to tell me I needed surgery. But I had heard too many bad things about back surgery, so that was out of the question. I said, "God will heal me without that."

Well, sometimes how you think God should do things is not what he is going to do at all. So I waited on my healing for almost a year. I got worse every day. I took pain pills by the handful. And I still hurt. Then I gave in. No, I didn't give up on God; I just realized he had a different plan. The doctors told me I would still be in pain and that I would need a walking device to help me get around and that I would never walk right again.

I told them, "God has the last say, and he will not leave me this way."

I made one doctor so mad he turned red. He said, "God doesn't have anything to do with this," and put my X-ray up in the light. "Do you see this?" he said.

I said, "Yes."

He replied, "Well, this is one of the worst cases I have seen. And you will be on pain pills for the rest of your life."

I refused to believe that. I told him, "My God is going to heal me." I left that doctor's office crying. My husband was in the middle; he tried all the way home to get me to see what the doctor was looking at because he had been doing back surgeries for almost thirty years.

That's why Jesus went to the cross; that's what his blood did for us. God gave us his only son so we could be healed. So I pray for each of you to stay strong and know his timing is not your timing. Anyway, I got the surgery in August 2002. I was supposed to be in the hospital for two weeks. I was only in there five days. The pain pills, I kicked them three days after coming home. No, it wasn't easy; nothing is very easy no matter how it sounds. But if it had not been for God, I would not have been able to do it. See, in this time, with all the pain, there were a couple times I picked up my pill bottles and poured them all in my hand, and then there was a voice that said, "Do it and all your pain will go away." Then a voice of truth said, "Think about what you will be losing. Your grandchildren will never know you. And your kids, who you have watched over and tried so hard to keep them from harm, how bad do you think this will hurt them to lose you?" And I cried out, "But I can't take the pain! It's more then I can bear."

I put the pills back. Then I got a call from my brother-in-law Jessie telling me to come to a church named Door of Hope. They were having a healing service. So we went. I didn't tell the people praying for others what was wrong with me. But they knew; they even knew where my back was broken. It took a lot of the pain away and made it easy to deal with. So see, just cry out to him when this world is too much. When you can't handle it, he will hear you and reach out his hand. But you have got to believe.

After my surgery, it was supposed to be about two years before I could return to even a part-time job. But ten months later, I returned to part-time work at a Tire and Lube shop. I have seen a lot of people headed for back surgery, and they don't realize I have had back surgery myself, because I don't use anything to help me get around, and I don't take pain pills. I'm just like you. If I overdo it, I will hurt, and yes, I do push myself a lot of times—just to be able to show that if it weren't for God, I would be in a wheelchair. So now my testimony is greater, and the people I tell come in with sadness and no hope, and they leave glad and filled with hope and joy that he still healing to this day. His plan is always better. You may not always understand until you get to the end of what you are going through, but know he won't let you do it alone. And don't give up because he doesn't do something the way you think he should. That is a big mistake a lot of people make. Don't be one of those people. Learn from my story and do better than me. Learn that early in life. That is when we found Door of Hope, when we were going though this. This church is like a family, a place I feel at home when I walk through the doors. It is a small church in Camden.

CHAPTER 8

A NEW HOME

*W*hen we settled with the trucking company, we decided to build a house. God works a lot through dreams, and when we decided to do this, he gave me a date that we would be moving in a dream. But just like Noah, we were laughed at, and Jeremy didn't want me telling my dreams from God because people were calling me crazy. Although Jeremy had seen my dreams come true, he didn't like people calling me that. But I didn't care. I would tell it anyway, so everyone would know it was God. We had to clear some land for it first. Well, God had given me a moving date two years before the time. And he helped us out by giving us some things at cheap prices along the way. I would go to the flea market and find things we needed, like a beautiful chandelier for two dollars, and there were other things like a $300 Christmas tree for only seventy-five dollars still in the box, never opened. So we got the land ready and then were waiting on them to get started. Two months went by, and they had not started. God told us to get our pastor to bless the land before we could build. And things kept getting put off until my husband got him out there to bless the land. It was just before Christmas. Everyone said, "There is no way you will move when you said you were." I said, "God gave me a moving date, and that is when I'm moving, no matter where it is." They made me feel like Noah in the Bible.

My moving date was the last weekend in March, the first weekend in April. God has a sense of humor because the last day of March was on Saturday, and the first day of April was Sunday. And we moved into our house that weekend. No one believed me that we would be moving. We didn't have to move far; we lived in a trailer on my mama and daddy's land. But our new home was on our own land that we had bought together, and the two lands are side by side. This was our first home together because the trailer was mine when Jeremy came into my life. So when God gives you a date, it will be that date. Just know that people who don't hear God when he is talking to them don't always understand.

And it makes you different from everyone, so be a Noah or a Moses. Let them talk about you, and when God shows up, he will shut them up.

Stand strong. The blood that covers me and covers you is Jesus's blood. He is where our strength comes from. He is our light in the dark. I pray that reading this makes you stronger and builds your faith to where you can overcome, because this world is not getting better.

CHAPTER 9

DOOR OF HOPE

*Y*ou must have a place to run to for peace. Most people find that at a church. And I love my church; I have seen the hand of God move there.

One time I got an infection in the right side of my face. It started at my ear, I went to the doctor, and she put me on meds and told me to come back in six days. I went on Thursday, and by Saturday, I was worse, so bad a nurse that comes to the shop told me I needed to go to the ER. See, it had moved into my face. I told her I had to work, that I had no time. I got off that Saturday at 1:00 p.m., went home, and got up the next morning for church. I was even worse than the day before, and my right eye was swollen shut. But God told me I would be healed at church. And let me tell you, I was looking for it everywhere; I went to the bathroom and put water on my face. I went to the front and prayed. I didn't know when or where in service that day my healing was going to come. But it would come before church even started.

My husband tried to get me to go to the ER, but I wouldn't go. I had to see what God was going to do at church. Well the pastor's wife came in. She saw me, and I told her the story. She too tried to get me to go to the ER, but I said, "No." Then the pastor came in.

He saw me and asked what happened. I told him. Well, he went to the front like he always did and put his stuff up and started praying. Then he came to me and said God told him to pray over my face. And while he was praying, there was a burning in the right side of my face. When he got done, he turned and started to walk away. I called out to him, "Pastor Gerald, look." He stopped and turned around. The swelling in my face was already going away by the time everyone got to church. It looked like nothing had happened. The swelling was gone, the redness, and he had only taken about three steps before I could see. It was amazing. God healed me right in front of him. I wore sunglasses into church that morning because I was ashamed that my face looked like I had been beaten, but I did not need them when I left. By the end of service, my face was back to normal.

The devil wanted me to go to the ER, and if I had, I would not have this wonderful story to tell how God is still opening blind eyes, because I couldn't see at all out of that eye. It was starting to go to the other side. I was glad I waited on God. But sometimes we grow tired of waiting and we give up. That's when you should reach your hands to the sky and cry out to Jesus. I promise he is there. He is waiting on you, just wanting you to call his name.

One of my favorite stories to tell happened to me at Door of Hope. It started the first Sunday in 2010. My friend from church and I prayed for grandchildren that Sunday. And afterwards, a young lady walking by asked us, "What are y'all up to?" We smiled and said we were praying for grandchildren. I didn't give it another thought. Then on February 21, 2010, a Sunday, I was in church, and during worship service I went somewhere else. There was a girl in front of me holding a baby, and a voice behind me called my name and said, "Here is your grandbaby." Then I was back in church. When I told my husband about what I saw and heard, he thought I was going crazy and made me promise not to tell anyone else about it. He wanted me to see a doctor. I told him, "I know what I saw, and I know what I heard." I wrote on a calendar, "God already told me about my grandbaby," so that whoever was giving me a grandchild would know it was from God. My husband was worried that wanting to be a grandmother had sent me off the deep end.

For almost three weeks, I watched my sons' girlfriends and my daughter. Then one night my daughter wanted to take me out to eat. My husband was on nightshift, so I said okay. Well, it ended up being the boys and one girlfriend. As we were sitting there laughing and cutting up, just having fun, they brought out our food. Jacob's girlfriend started to take a bite, but then she got sick and ran to the bathroom. I had been watching all this time, and here it was. God reminded me of what he showed me at church. I got excited, and my youngest son got upset with me because of the excitement. I told him, "You don't know what I know, son." Then she came back, and I asked if she was okay, and she said, "I'm fine." So we all went on like nothing happened. We left and headed home, and on the way, I called my husband and told him, "I know who is having a baby," and I told him what happened. We talked all the way home. He tried to talk me out of it; I tried to talk him into it.

Anyway, I got home and was trying to figure out how I was going to tell them they were going to have a baby. At that point, the only person who knew about God telling me about my grandbaby coming was the love of my life, my husband, Jeremy, and he thought I was crazy. Then lights came through my window. I looked out, and it was them. I was on the house phone with my husband. I told him they were there, and he said, "What are you going to say?"

"I don't know," I replied.

So I opened the door. My son still a little upset with me. He said, "So, Mama, I want to know why you were so happy to see her sick." She said, "It's okay, not a big deal." He said, "Yes it is." I looked at them and just started telling the story to them. I ended with, "You're carrying my grandbaby." My son said, "Wait a minute. What? This is not what I was looking for." I said, "I can prove it." He asked what I was smoking that I thought I could prove I talked to God. I showed them the calendar and where I wrote, "God already told me." I told her to go to the doctor. This was on a Monday, and she got an appointment on Wednesday. They came to my work to let me know she was going to have a baby. She was about a week when God told me about my granddaughter. And the story doesn't end there. The young lady that walked by us, her little girl was born at the end September. My granddaughter was born October 28, 2010, and my friend's granddaughter was born in November.

This story shows the truth from Matthew 18:20 about where two or more are gathered with a pure heart. Both of us love the Lord. By now, your faith should have gone up. You must feel him around you. He is there by your side, in the darkest moments of your life, when it seems the world is closing in and it seems you are all alone. He is there.

We all have those times that we hide from everyone else. Well you can't hide from God. One time my daddy was sick, and he is not one to go to the doctor. I woke up at 3:50 a.m. and was crying and talking to God. I talked to him about my mama and daddy, I talked to him about my kids and the path they were on and my granddaughter and her mama. See, my son had stepped outside of his marriage, and his wife had taken the only grandbaby I knew and a little girl that could be my grandchild. I thanked him for everything he had done. I had a coworker who had a grandson that was born and in the hospital, not doing well. This was on a Wednesday morning. I talked to him about my husband. We were going through a rough time in our marriage; we were also upside down, it seemed, going two different ways. I wasn't sure we were going to make it, but we didn't give up. So at this time I felt so alone and like my world was falling apart. I told God I had no one I could really talk to, because no one seemed to understand me, and being alone made me feel like an outsider. I cried and poured my heart out to him.

That night at church, a lady come to me and asked, "Are you okay?" I said, "Yes, ma'am," and she said, "Are you sure you're okay?" I said. "Yes, ma'am. Why?" She said, "God woke me up at four o'clock this morning and had me pray for you. He showed me pictures of an elderly couple, a newborn baby I've never seen before, all three of your kids, and he showed me your Jeremy, but I didn't understand that part. Because he was far from you, and you were crying."

I burst into tears and told her I was sorry God woke her up for me, to show me that I meant so much to him he wanted me to know he heard my every cry. Then I began to tell her everything.

In 2011, I prayed again around March for Jeanette. Then my next granddaughter was born in January 2012. But it was not by Jeanette; it was a young lady I didn't even know at the time. That was an answer to prayers, but with her, I was kept from her for two years. See, they are sisters. It was a rough time for my oldest two granddaughters. They didn't even know each other, and it would be a year before they met. See, their mothers were best friends in school, which made this more of a mess. Prayers go a long way, and God answered me and let me into her life. I did not know the pain I would go through to be in her life.

See, my daughter-in-law took her from us and didn't want us to have anything to do with her. I asked, "God, why should I lose one granddaughter just to be with the other? It's not fair."

See, we all go though things. When we turn to God, we ask, "God, why are you doing this to me? Don't you know my heart? I love you, and I thought you loved me too. So I don't understand this." My son was torn to pieces; he didn't know what to do. We weren't sure at the time if the baby was his, but we soon found out she was. God doesn't make mistakes; he knew the whole time how this was going to play out. Well, nine months before my oldest granddaughter's third birthday, a lady I think a lot of gave her a pony for her third birthday. I tried to tell her I didn't know anything about horses or ponies. But she said that it had been on her heart and mind for two months. So I built a pen for him. I didn't understand why God gave her this pony. But by her third birthday, her mama had taken her and moved far away from us. I was trying to be strong for my son, but I felt like a failure. See, to be strong for someone else, you first have to get strength for yourself from God. And this sure showed me I was not as strong as I thought. Everyone said to me, "Why are you so torn? You are only the grandmother." But you see, I lost more than a grandchild. My son, my daughter-in-law, my world was upside down. I wanted to know if this baby was my grandchild. So I cried at work, in the car, at church, basically everywhere. Even at the store.

One night, I was crying in a store and saw a young pastor and told him what was going on. He wanted to pray for her to come back to Door of Hope. I told him, "That is what I want, so that is not what I want prayed for." I wanted him to pray for her to end up in the church God had planned for her, not me. What I had been praying for was coming, but I couldn't see past the pain of the loss. People at Door of Hope won't push into what you are going through unless God sends them to you.

We wait on God there, because if God isn't in it, then it isn't God. So three weeks before her birthday, God whispered to me while I was working and told me three things.

1. I was to prepare to have my granddaughter from Friday to Sunday.
2. I would start to have her a week at a time.
3. There was also a message to my son. (I told him what God told me to tell him, and it also to came true. But that is between him and God, not for me to tell.)

After God told me this, I went to three people to find a babysitter. Everyone told me that there was no way that would happen. So two Sundays passed, and Pastor Brown was preaching. He stopped, called me out, told me stop crying, and said, "God said he has already given you your answer," which made me cry that much more. I had my answer, but I didn't know when.

That Monday, my sister-in-law Jenny stopped by my work out of the blue to check on me. I started crying and told her everything, so she stood with me and agreed that what I heard from God would come true. So then my granddaughter's birthday came, and she did get to come to her birthday party and get her pony. So my daughter-in-law did let us have her the next week from Saturday to Sunday.

When she left, I cried to God and told him, "This is not what you told me." I was upset and crying, and I prayed to God to forgive me for that. I told him I was sorry. That week, my daughter-in-law called me and told me she felt guilty. I told her she had no reason for that. She told me not about Jacob but about me. So she told me, "I know you work on Saturday, but if you will meet me halfway, then you can get her on Friday after work and keep her until Sunday at 7:00 p.m." See, she had moved two hours away to Charleston.

So God already knew how that year was going to go, and it changed me. It made me stronger. Because that was not going to be the only time her mama tried to take us out of her life. And it wasn't because she is a mean person but because she was hurt and though that she herself had been replaced, and she didn't want to be hurt any more. But with God on my side, who can be against me? That's why you love him with your heart, not your mouth. It is easy to say, "I love you," even if it isn't in your heart.

For the first year of knowing about my youngest granddaughter, we had to keep them apart, and my heart was so heavy over this. And God knew it. I planned a family trip to Florida but was going to have to leave her out. Then, just in time, God kicked the door down and opened up the windows to where the girls could be together, and no one could ever keep them apart again no matter what. And the sister love they have for each other is so strong; I've never seen a bond so close. When God did this, I felt a freedom I had lost a long time ago. The chains that were broken, the load that was taken, it was amazing. The hurt and anger that my oldest granddaughter's mama felt, I wish I could take it from her. I too know the pain and the hurt my son did. But would I change anything if I could? No, I wouldn't change one hair on either one of their heads. Not even who their mothers are. I can see why my son was taken by both young ladies. I would have chosen them too for him, but God chose them first. Both are good mothers, and I love them both no matter what they do to hurt me, or try to take me out of my granddaughters' lives. I know it truly is not them at all.

As you read on, you will see him answer ever prayer.

This life we live in is not our own to do with what we want to do. We are to do the best we can and be the best at what God has us here for. People will give up on you easily. You make one mistake, and they put you in the bad apple barrel. Just remember one thing: the first ones to talk junk are the ones with the most junk hiding in their closet. God knows we are not perfect. That's why his son went to the cross. So we would have a chance. Without Jesus, we don't stand a chance at all. And remember, it doesn't matter what the world thinks of you; it is what God thinks of you. And Jesus was thinking of you when he was on that cross. These are just some stories to show you how God has always been there for me.

CHARTER 10

STORMS

*Y*our world can crumble around you in a minute. Trust me; no one in this world has it figured out. No amount of money, no amount of worldly goods can stop a storm. Just like the land needs the rain, we too need a storm in our lives, and yes, it seems like some storms are never going to end. But no matter how little or big, God always has a rainbow at the end. I'm no different. I have had my share of storms. Some made me feel alone, and some made me want to take my life, but none were strong enough to make me turn from God.

In this chapter, I hope and pray you find that I didn't think I was as strong as God, but I found God was there. See, God has more faith in us than we have in ourselves. The world likes to tell us, "You can't do that." Don't listen to what the world says; it will only kick you when you are down.

When I was in school, I was one that got picked on. There was this group of girls that was picking on me and my sister, and we was only in the eighth grade. They were in ninth and tenth grade. We were not big girls at that time. These girls were twice our size. We were on the bus, and the tenth grader started calling us names. I had enough, so I stood up to her. I told her to stop calling us names and whatever names she said about us went for her and her sister. She stood up and knocked me down. I stood right back up, ready to fight, but she laughed at me and sat back down. By then, the whole bus was laughing. Back then, fights on the bus weren't reported; it was considered off school property. Standing up for yourself is not easy; as a matter of fact, you may do like I did with that girl. There were two licks; she hit me, and I hit the floor. Yes, it is a funny story, but it wasn't at the time. God was already teaching me to stand up to someone bigger than me, even then. He knew what I would face in a few more years. And you can't win a war without training. I knew I couldn't win, but I was tired of being picked on.

Two days later, the next girl in line came for me, but this time I had more fight in me. She sat on the back of the seat in front of me and accused me of trying to talk to her boyfriend. I tried to tell her I wasn't, but she hit me anyway, and she had put rings on every finger. But you see, I didn't go down as easily as she thought I would. By the time the bus stopped, she was begging for someone to get me off of her. Our bus driver pulled me off of her. So do your best in school. Don't let others make you give up on school. I would find every reason I could not to go to school because of the meanness. I got picked on and teased so badly I hated to go to school, and my grades showed it.

Just so you know, you don't have to be grown to have a storm in your life. Your life storms can start at any age. It is how you handle yourself when you are going through hard times because, at the end of the day, one way or another, you will be changed. You will come out stronger than before or weaker.

So be careful what you pray for; it too can lead to a storm. When I was fifteen years old, all I wanted was love. Well I thought I found it. I told you in the beginning about how my first husband and how it turned out.

The heart is a funny thing and the most dangerous part of you. Your heart opens you up and sets you up to be toyed with by the opposite sex. The storm I would find myself in would last on and off eight and a half years. He played mind games, he and his family in this storm.

I found a love that never failed me, would not play mind games, and would always tell me the truth no matter how badly it hurt me. That love was Jesus Christ. He was always there to pick me up and dust me off. And my kids and I built our world around the four of us. I knew God had us. Life is not easy, and the younger you start trying to be grown, the harder it is. Because in this world today, you are too young to do anything if you are under twenty-one, even to get a good job. This is not to make you feel sorry for me but to help you understand why I am so in love with my God and my Jesus. And I pray that you love him from your heart, your whole heart, by the time you finish reading this book.

These stories are from me so that God is not left out, because he has played a big role in my life.

I have tried to fit in with others. Sometimes some people just don't fit in anywhere. I happen to be one of those, so my friends were few, and boyfriends were even fewer. I did not want to let my mama and daddy down, and I didn't want to disappoint my father. I wanted to be a good person, and like any teenage girl, I wanted friends and boyfriends, but it seemed like I was the poster child for getting picked on. In my life, I have come to understand one thing: those who pick on others do it to make themselves feel better. They don't like themselves at all.

I pray you are wiser than me. I didn't do what everyone else did. That alone made me an outcast—the smoking, drugs, and drinking. I wanted no part of that world. But just because someone does those things, we don't judge them. We pray for Jesus to help them.

Everyone has to find Jesus in their own way and their own timing. Remember, we all do things we pray no one finds out about. You help a person by your life for Jesus in front of others, telling them what he has done for you. When someone is in sinful life and they talk about how much fun they are having, it is because of all they are trying to forget. Just know that there is no pain, no problem you will face in your life that God doesn't understand. He told me to write this for you. So when someone comes at you, put

God in front. And in the end, there are two kinds of people that come out of storms.

1. A better person
2. A bitter person

You will hear bad things happen to good people. Well let me tell you something: we are all bad right from the get go. We have to work at being good because there are traps everywhere. Just remember, God is on our side, so that means we can overcome the traps set for us. God wants us to be happy; it is this world that stands in our way.

I have always been out of place here in this world. When I had my three kids, I thought, *I will finally have someone that I will have something in common with*. Nope, life doesn't work out the way you plan. You can make all the plans you want, but if they don't line up with what God has planed, then your plans will end up on a backburner.

Turns out they all kind of act more like Jeremy than me. I'm still alone. My husband tells me all the time there is no one like me. I believe it. My kids and now my grandkids are my world. I wrap myself up in them and need them to keep me going.

I found myself in a storm with one of my grandchildren when I found out there was a chance my youngest son could have another child out there. I wanted a DNA test but was told that it could never happen or I would lose the only granddaughter I had. I cried. I didn't want to lose one granddaughter. My daughter-in-law and son agreed he would not push to find out if she was his daughter. See, it was hard for her because it was her best friend that had the baby, but I didn't want one granddaughter to grow up without me either. So I poured out my heart to God and told him I didn't want her to be twenty-two and standing on my doorstep wondering where I was her whole life. I understood my daughter-in-law's point. But from a grandmother's point, I wanted to know, and if I pushed it, the result would be I would never see my oldest granddaughter again. Let me tell you now, watch what you pray for, because sometimes the answer comes with a lot of pain. Almost two years passed, and the young lady pushed for a DNA test. She gave up rights for child support; all she wanted was her daughter to know her family. I had no part in her pushing for the test that proved I had two granddaughters.

People would show me pictures of a little girl and tell me, "This is your other granddaughter." I would tell them to tell her mama to get a DNA test. I would tell them to tell her how much she was cheating her by not getting it. So she finally did, and when she did, my daughter-in-law took my granddaughter from us. But God had already started working on getting my granddaughter back. See at the beginning of the year, a lady I know who only knew my granddaughter by pictures came to me and said she wanted to give her a pony for her third birthday. All we had to do was build a pen for him. Just as we got the pen finished, my daughter-in-law took my granddaughter and left. She kept her from us for two months. She wanted to cancel the birthday party with the pony, but we couldn't. I had already sent out invitations, and I prayed she would change her mind. And she did; it was two and a half months since I had seen her. That's how God got her back into our lives. The DNA test came back, and the little girl was his. I was crying out to God, "It wasn't supposed to turn out like this." I wanted both granddaughters right here in the same town with me. The pain I was feeling I know wasn't as bad as my son's pain. But the world still turned, the sun still came up, we still had to work. Pain doesn't stop life; I found it still goes on with you or without you.

When your heart is in a million pieces, Jesus is the only one who can put them back in place. I cried for my oldest granddaughter because she was taken from me, and I cried over my other granddaughter, because she was kept from me. I prayed over them both.

CHAPTER 11

THE HURTS OF LIFE

*P*eople will tell you the hurts make you who you are, and that might be so, but I say a lot of the hurts you go through are for someone in your future that you need to help. Because they will not be strong enough to go though it alone, and you won't understand without going through it. So you never know when God has it for you or someone else, but either way, you will get something out of it. I have had lots of stormy nights when I didn't think the sun was going to come up and I didn't want it to. So don't think you are the only one that life is hard on. No matter what comes at you, God has you in his arms. If you have read this book, then you already know God has always been with me, but I did not always think so.

There were times when I felt alone even in a room full of people, thinking I did not want life to go on for me anymore. And the storm I was in was one of my hardest.

It showed me that I would fall apart if one of my kids went out on their own. They needed to try things out for themselves and cut themselves off from me. I cried all the time, the worst thing a parent can go through, not knowing if their child is okay or hurt lying in a ditch somewhere, out of their mind, or if they need something to eat. Jacob felt like he needed to get away; he cut me out of his life.

He was going from one home to another to sleep. This tore me up because he was only seventeen years old. And things of this world had a hand on him. I had people telling me to give up on him, to let him go because he was lost. And I told those people, "How I can give up on him when God never gave up on me? This is my son, my baby." To turn my back on him was no option.

Then God gave me a word to text to his phone even if he didn't text back: Baal Perazim. You can find it in 2 Samuel 5:20. And because of this, it was only a few weeks before he showed up on my doorstep in the middle of the night. He was sick and wanted to come home. I let him in and told him the rules had not changed but this was his home. Then he asked, "What is that you have been texting me?" I laughed and said, "God told me to text you that. It means to beat the enemies with God's own hand." He told me later that made him want to come home. So when you pray over your kids, God is listening. In this time while he was trying to find himself, I felt like I was losing myself. I'm not much on family, but when it comes to my kids, they keep me here. Just remember, it doesn't matter who your parents are or if you even know them; you have a father in heaven that loves you more than you can imagine, God the father, and he talks to you every day even if you don't talk to him. God doesn't make mistakes, and he knows if you're not married. In the Bible, there are more women in there than you realize who got pregnant out of wedlock. But people don't talk about that part of the Bible; they will put young people down for this when they don't have room to. That is just people being in other people's business, so they will tell you the right thing to do is get married. That might be the last thing God wants you to do. I'm not saying go out and get pregnant; that's turning my words around. Always follow God. Do a better job than I did. Maybe things would have been better if I had been closer to God as a teenager. Looking back at so many crossroads in my life, I wonder how many times I chose wrong. I won't know till I stand before God. So my fight for my kids started long before they were born. And anyone who knows me knows one thing to leave alone is my kids—and yes, to this day, I pray over them that God will watch over them even when I can't.

I'm not perfect. I held my kids close. The whole world was out to get me and to hurt me; that's what was playing in my mind. The devil will use your own mind against you. It is a playing field, and he is good at mind games. So I thought people would hurt my kids to hurt me, and my first husband did that very thing. See, he had no love for them or me. I have always felt alone and like it was me against the world. When I did have kids, I thought I would have someone like me so I wouldn't be alone; that wasn't the case at all. I'm forty-five, and I'm telling you I still have loneliness, because this world is not my home, and I long for home. This world offers nothing but heartache and pain. And I don't like to focus on that part of my life. Focusing on all the hurt, pain, disappointment, and loss that comes from this world will make you lose your mind. This world is hard enough without that focus. Your focus should be on the good. Try to forget the rest, even though you will find it overwhelming at times. That is this world stealing your joy. Hold your hands up when thing are so bad that you are crying and just say, "I love you, Lord Jesus, and if this pain is in your will, then I know I will be okay, because you are with me, and you will help me through this."

Anyway, I have so much to say, and I want to make sure you see God in everything in this book. The words are from him; this whole book is from him. God's love is more than you can dream of. And he didn't make you or me for someone to mistreat. Or just leave when it starts. Anyway, the blood of Jesus covers you, so don't be afraid. When you have his blood covering you, you are safe from even yourself. Like the way he stepped in and stopped me from murdering my first husband. When he beat me at the age of eighteen, if God had not stepped in, I would not have had my youngest son. So I am grateful to him for all the mistakes he saved me from. I get mad when people blame God for the bad things in their life and all the things going wrong, because if people would listen to him, it would never get that bad. God loves us; he is not this mean, vindictive God. He loves and cares; we make it hard on ourselves and then blame him.

Why? Because we are too busy to be still and wait and listen to what he has to say. But he has written a book telling us what not to do. It is called the Bible. And what does every one do? The opposite of it. Yes, even me. I have not always done right. It took me eight and a half years, off and on, to realize God had better for me.

This world makes it hard to find what God has for you. But just know God is the same now as he was two thousand years ago. In this fast world, we find it hard to hear him, but he also leaves signs. You have to know him to be able to follow them. God's love is the truest you will find; he wants nothing from you but your love back. See, he already has everything, so there is nothing left to give him but yourself. But we have to choose him, and make no mistake, I know he knows my name, and with knowing that, he knows my kids' and my grandkids' names.

It is hard trying to date when you have kids. You don't want to bring everyone that comes into your life into their little lives. I was so glad when I met the man God had for me. He was everything I asked for. This was the man I prayed for. I'm not saying we have a perfect marriage. I don't think there is such a thing, and marriage brings a lot of heartache and brokenness to the table. Would I do it all over again if I knew then what I know now? Yes. Even though when I'm mad at my husband I tell him differently. Life with him has not been as easy as I would like, but life is better with him than without him. Young men, let God guide you to the girl he has for you. And until then, treat any girl you are with like you love her. Don't be a cruel man. Be kind and gentle. Be there for her.

Young women, don't chase a man. I don't care how good he is, how much you love him. You are a treasure because God said so, and if he can't see that in you, then he is not the one God has for you. Let him leave. God will never fail you. As long as you have God, you can make it on your own. Don't be like me and wait almost nine years to see you're not alone. Don't let anyone run over you or run you down. God did not make us for that. Too many people look down out of shame when they could look up and have it washed away.

Now three years into our marriage, we wanted to have a baby.

I had been fixed where I couldn't have any more, so we went to the doctor, and I had a miscarriage. God was there for me through that as well. It was very painful. I didn't think the pain would ever stop. I would cry every time I saw a newborn baby. But I finally got peace, knowing they are with God and they know how much I love them. The night before going to the doctor to get my babies put back in, I had a dream the doctor came out and told me she needed to talk to me. She took me to a room where she began to tell me three of my babies had died the night before, and I only had four left. She wanted to know if I wanted to do all four or freeze two and do two. I did all four. Well, when I got to the doctor's office, the dream had come true, but I ended up miscarrying all four. They would have been born in June 2001. Why did God take them from me? I don't know. Did I get mad at God? No. Maybe the pain will help someone close to me so I can understand something they go through.

Then when my kids were grown, they went through their phases of shutting me out. That just tore me apart inside. They were in a place they didn't want to talk to me or see me. I would pray over them. I would send them a text telling them I love them even if I didn't get anything back. I knew they were in a dark place and needed me more than they ever did. My text would say, "I love you, and no matter what, you are still my child, and you still can come home when you get ready." I would never turn my back on my children. I am where I am because God never turned his back on me. No matter what I did or said, he was there for me. So for me to turn my back on my child was out of the question, no matter what people said. So many people told me I was a fool for texting and calling and told me I should give up on them. But I don't look at things the way others do. See, I thought, what if God felt that way about me and gave up on me? Where would I be today? I am no more special than you or anyone else in this evil world. God talks to us all, but so does the devil, so you have to be careful who you lesson to. If you can hear one's voice, you will surely hear the other's, and yes, I don't like to talk about it, but I do hear voices, and I have found out it is hereditary. So be careful who you lesson to. The devil is deceitful. He will try to make you think he is from God. So then my children found their way home just before I went crazy. Then all the people that said I should give up had to shut up, and some were mad that God answered my cries. Yes, I cried every night while I prayed for God to watch over them, because I couldn't see them, but he knew where they were and what they were doing even if I didn't. All I knew was my world was empty without them. And he would always bring them home. They think it was their idea. I never tried to control them. I just don't want to be shut off from them.

Let me tell you a story. My oldest son left and went and stayed with his girlfriend's parents. Things weren't right there. I had people coming to me, telling me I needed to get him out of there, but when your kids are grown or think they are, you have to love them enough to let them make their own mistakes. All you can do is pray that God will watch over them. Well, I was at the Laundromat when my cell phone rang. Funny thing is my phone never got service there. I didn't recognize the number, but I answered anyway. It was the people my son Steven was living with. They were trying to call him; they didn't even dial my number. But God had a plan to show my son who they really were. See, all the things that I had been told about what they were doing to my son, I got my chance to ask them about it. I had been told they had him selling drugs and stealing doing, things I knew was wrong.

We stayed on the phone about one and a half hours. So after all that time on the phone with them, I told them, "Have a good day and tell my son I love him."

Well, they told my son I called them cussing and raising cane. They didn't know me. See, everything they told him I said, Steven knew me well enough to know his mama didn't talk that way. He didn't think I had their number, and he was right. So that weekend, he finally came to see me. And I was so glad to see him; I had not seen him in a month. It was his birthday, and I had made him a birthday dinner. And after dinner, my three kids and I were sitting in the living room, laughing and talking, having a great time. Then out of the blue, he said, "Mama, I need to ask you about something. Where did you get the number to call the people I live with?"

I said, "Son, I don't have their number."

He said, "But you called them last week."

I said, "No I didn't. They called me looking for you."

He said, "But they don't have your number."

I'm not good at clearing my phone, which was a good thing at that time. I went and got my phone and showed him where they called me and how much time we talked. Then he started telling me what they said I said, and I took out all the add-on and told him what I really said. As he sat there telling his brother and sister what was said, they said, "Can you really see Mama saying that?" I just shook my head that they lied on me the way they did. I still don't understand the reason behind it. But that day he left, went there, got his stuff, and came home. Then two weeks later in church at Door of Hope, someone stood up and told a story.

How someone they needed to talk to had called them but didn't dial their number. So I stood up and told my story so they could see that sometimes when God wants two people to talk, it doesn't matter if they don't know each other's phone number. Prayers can be answered with redirect calls, because cell phone calls are made in the air; there is no line anymore. So don't think God isn't in everything, because he is. God's son, Jesus, didn't go to the cross to take away power. Jesus went to the cross to give power back, but it is up to us to use it. And it starts with where your heart belongs. Who does your life reflect that lives within you? I think everyone should see him in everything because he is everywhere. The things I tell that have to do with my kids, I only tell my part; they have their own story to tell what happened. I'm not afraid of anything or anyone in this world, because Jesus is with me all the time, and I tell my kids, "Don't make me get my ten thousand angels on you." The only thing that scares me is losing one of my kids or grandkids. Or someone keeping one of my grandchildren from me, and I know God won't let that happen. I tell my grandchildren, "If I have to fight to stay in your life, you better believe I will fight with ever breath in my body. God would not give you to me to turn my back on you."

Too many parents of young men turn away from their grandchildren, because the baby's mama doesn't want anything to do with him or his family. And like my lawyer told me one time, some will made a big deal over nothing just to make the daddy and his family say this is not worth the hassle; they will wait till their grandchildren are grown. That's not the way God made families to be. I would give my last breath to stay in my grandchildren's life. I will never walk away. And by the grace of God, the fights won't take long.

The devil wants me out of my granddaughters' lives because they are going to grow up and be Godly women. They will be strong. They already are strong, and to be so young, the hurt and pain that they are going through, when they reach the age to do what God has for them to do, there will be no stopping them. My oldest granddaughter already hears from him. One morning, my daughter called. Her car was broken down, and she needed her daddy to go get her. My granddaughter said, "Wait, Papa. Take this to my aunt NetNet." It was a candle in the shape of a star. When they got back, my daughter asked why she sent it to her. I told her to go ask her niece. She did, and the answer she got was not what she was looking for. My granddaughter told her, "God told me to give it to you for something you said." See, Jeanette writes everything down in a notebook, the way she feels. Two nights earlier, she wrote down that she felt alone in a dark room with no light and that no one could hear her crying, not even God. She was hurting over words people had said to her, and that can make you feel alone and by yourself. So be careful of hurting people you love because love can turn to hate; that's why we should not do hurtful things to others.

Always find God in everything good or bad. Come out of bad things a better person, not bitter. Love like there is no tomorrow, because we don't know our last today. Don't hurt people because you are hurting; that's when you cry out to Jesus. He holds every tear in his hand. He knows your hurt better than you do. Don't ever give credit to the devil, for anything; he doesn't deserve it. Be strong enough to stand up for Jesus against anyone, because Jesus will always have your back even if you can't see him. There will be times you can't feel him, but he is there for you no matter what.

I have felt those feelings too, so you're not in this alone, in thinking he is not there. I'm telling you, God is not dead; he is alive and with you every day.

CHAPTER 12

BLESSINGS

I got sick in December 2014 and missed two days of work. I had worked for Tire and Lube shop for eleven years and had not missed work for being sick. My boss doesn't pay sick leave. Anyway I couldn't miss work but was so sick I had no choice.

I knew my check would be short, and we didn't know what we were going to do. I came back to work really early. I shouldn't have, but I couldn't stay out any longer. Then that Friday, when I got my check, it was $170 short. That afternoon, this couple pulled up and dropped off a car to get tires. Then they left and went to the store. They came back an hour later, and the car wasn't ready yet. They were sitting in their truck when she got out and called me to her. I said, "It is almost done. Not long now."

She said, "That's fine. I need to give you something."

I said, "Okay, what is it?" She reached out to me with money in her hand. And I said, "I can't take that."

She said, "You have to." Then she went on to tell me how every year they bless someone for Christmas, and she thought it was going to be one of her coworkers, and God told her, "No, not them." So they thought a random person at the store, so they had went to the store and walked all over, and everyone they asked about, "Is that them?" God would say, "No." They got back to the shop and were sitting in the truck trying to find out where God wanted them to go with the money.

So she looked at me and said, "God said that's who you give it to. So you have to take it."

I started crying and told her, "I was sick at the first of the week, and my boss don't pay sick leave, so my check was short." When I counted it, it was $200. God gave me more, so see, he love us. And just know I love you even if you are reading this after I'm gone and you can't see me, and you can't talk to me, where I can't answer you face to face, but I am always with you.

And that is how Jesus loves us to. Jesus does talk to us all. You just have to listen with your heart, because he doesn't yell; he whispers. His voice is not like any other. So when you are at a crossroad, and you don't know what to do, be still, and he will guide you. So here is something God told me a long time ago.

What is it you don't think I have done for you?

What would you sacrifice for your spouse, children, or even your grandchildren?

I have already sacrificed everything for you and them.

Your sacrifice for them will not work, only from the heart and from you as well.

They will learn from your sacrifice what to do.

Then they will know how to sacrifice to me.

I was in a bad place when he gave this to me. I was trying so hard to do everything for me and my kids, and doing things in my kids' names, and he showed me I can't do that. He sees everything, he knows everything, and there is no fooling him. So see, everyone has to find him on their own. I wish I could save you from the heartache and pain of this world, but I can't. All I can do is write my story and pray it helps you. I pray you find that being hurtful to others, because you are hurting, is not a way to be. A kind word may save a life and give someone on the edge a little hope that God does care. Like God said, "If someone is already mad, harsh words will only make it worse." Your love and words reflect your heart and what is really there.

God loves us. There isn't a page in the Bible you can't turn to that he doesn't tell you so. His words are there for everyone to see, but what does your word say?

God also tells us, "Don't be rash with your words" (Ecclesiastes 5:1–3), but read on to 5:9.

Words reflect love and faith or hate and disbelief. Every time you speak to someone new or someone you haven't seen in a while, they judge you on the first words that come out your mouth.

There are two ways of talking:

1. God's way
2. The devil's way

God doesn't care about the outside of you; it is what's inside that counts the most. And it starts with the heart. From your heart, you speak in your words, and you show who lives inside you. A person with strong faith has strong love. A person with strong disbelief has strong hate. And they may not realize it, how much they hate. So they use words to hurt before being hurt. They haven't had someone show them how much God loves each of us. God wants us to know what is really in our hearts. When we say, "I love you," a person can tell if it is true, and when you pray for someone, they can feel how strong your faith is. A prayer is only as strong as your faith. It's time for people to stand up and let God free us so we can do what he wants to do in our lives. So he can send us out to free others. Because if we have chains, how can we free anyone else? Our words will tell us where we stand. Just listen to yourself and how you talk around everyone.

God says, "What is in your heart will come out of your mouth" (Matthew 15:18–20). Words of love and faith go hand and hand. Be real. Stop hiding in the shadows, let God's love take over your heart, and feel the love like never before. Let him break those chains in your heart.

Please understand there is a fine line between light and dark, heaven and hell, love and hate, and only one lives inside of you. You can fool people; it is easy to do. But God knows what is truly in your heart and what lives there. God is waiting for us to wake up and come out of the shadows and come into his arms. Embrace his love and show the world that he is your Lord. God wants you to lean on him no matter what's going on in your life. And when you're in a valley, your hands are raised high to him, just as if you're on the mountaintop. Because God and only God can make a mountain into a valley. God wants us to be able to say, "I love you freely and truly." What does God's love mean to you? When was the last time you said to him, "I love you," from the heart? And remember, he knows the truth of what is there. God wants us to love each other as he loves us.

Think about this. How much easier is it to love someone you know nothing about? Okay now how about someone you know that no matter how nice you are or how good you try to be to them, they are just as hateful as they can be, and they say hateful words to try to hurt you for no reason.

These are the people God wants us to open our hearts to. Let his words come out and show them his love. People like this don't know how wonderful God is. They don't realize Jesus died for them too, so I ask you today, how and where do your words touch a person? Does it lift them up or tear them down? So always let that light shine on the outside that lives on the inside. And here is some scripture to go along with everything I have written.

Back in 2010, God would give me a Bible verse. I would write it down and study it. Then after about four months, he told me to put them together in the order he gave them to me. Well, I just didn't have time to do it.

So I got Jeanette, my daughter, to do it for me. When she finished, she came to me and said, "Mama, this is kind of harsh. Have you read this?"

I said, "Yes, it is Bible verses that God has given me to read over the last few months."

She said, "No. Read them together." I did, and just so everyone knows, each time I was given one of these, I was going through a lot of pain from someone hurting me with words and actions. And each one of these gave me comfort. So here is the letter God gave me in 2010. Read the next page as a letter. You will see what God thinks about people being mean.

Ye hypocrites, well did Esaias prophesy of you, saying,
This people draweth nigh unto me with their mouth,
and honoureth me with their lips; but their heart is far
from me. But in vain they do worship me, teaching for
doctrines the commandments of men. (Matthew 15:7–9)

And he said, I will hide my face from them, I will see what
their end shall be: for they are a very forward generation,
children in whom is no faith. (Deuteronomy 32:20)

For the sin of their mouth and the words of their lips
let them even be taken in their pride: and for cursing
and lying which they speak. (Psalm 59:12)

But the Lord said unto Samuel, Look not on his countenance, or
on the height of his stature; because I have refused him: for the
Lord seeth not as man seeth; for man looketh on the outward
appearance, but the Lord looketh on the heart. (1 Samuel 16:7)

As the Father hath loved me, so have I loved you: continue
ye in my love. If ye keep my commandments, ye shall abide
in my love; even as I have kept my Father's commandments,
and abide in his love. These things have I spoken unto you,
that my joy might remain in you, and that your joy might be
full. This is my commandment, That ye love one another,
as I have loved you. Greater love hath no man than this, that
a man lay down his life for his friends. (John 15:9–13)

But the fruit of the Spirit is love, joy, peace, longsuffering, gentleness, goodness, faith. Meekness, temperance: against such there is no law. And they that are Christ's have crucified the flesh with the affections and lusts. If we live in the Spirit, let us also walk in the Spirit. Let us not be desirous of vain glory, provoking one another, envying one another. (Galatians 5:22–26)

For the love of money is the root of all evil: which while some coveted after, they have erred from the faith, and pierced themselves through with many sorrows. But thou, O man of God, flee these things; and follow after righteousness, godliness, faith, love, patience, meekness. (1 Timothy 6:10–11)

A man shall eat good by the fruit of his mouth: but the soul of the transgressors shall eat violence. He that keepeth his mouth keepeth his life: but he that openeth wide his lips shall have destruction. (Proverbs 13:2–3)

A soft answer turneth away wrath: but grievous words stir up anger. The tongue of the wise useth knowledge aright: but the mouth of fools poureth out foolishness. (Proverbs 15:1–2)

But let us, who are of the day, be sober, putting on the breastplate of faith and love; and for an helmet, the hope of salvation. (1 Thessalonians 5:8)

Peace be to the brethren, and love with faith, from God the Father and the Lord Jesus Christ. Grace be with all them that love our Lord Jesus Christ in sincerity. Amen. (Ephesians 6:23–24)

My doctrine shall drop as the rain, my speech shall distil as the dew, as the small rain upon the tender herb, and as the showers upon the grass. (Deuteronomy 32:2)

That Christ may dwell in your hearts by faith; that ye,
being rooted and grounded in love. (Ephesians 3:17)

There is a way which seemeth right unto a man, but the
ends thereof are the ways of death. (Proverbs 14:12)

And the grace of our Lord was exceeding abundant with
faith and love which is in Christ Jesus. (1 Timothy 1:14)

Let the words of my mouth, and the meditation of
my heart, be acceptable in thy sight, O LORD, my
strength, and my redeemer. (Psalm 19:14)

Set a watch, O LORD, before my mouth; keep
the door of my lips. (Psalm 141:3)

I am not a person who knows the Bible well. Yes, I do read it, and I do look to find answers there sometimes—some kind of hope or a kind word to make sense of this world. But to say I know it well enough to get those verses on my own, there is no way. To me, reading them all together like a letter tells you not to be mean to one other. That is not what God wants us to do. And it lets us know not to love him with our mouths but with our hearts. You cannot fool him. See, he made each of you, so he knows the truth about you. God gave the verses to me, and then I showed the letter to others, and people wanted copies of this because they never knew this was in the Bible. Make your everyday living reflect that what Jesus has done for you and me was not done in vain.

His death means something to you. That cross is not just for one person. And in my lowest times, I am so grateful that my God is not dead. And know one more thing about me: I would give my life for my Jesus. I pray I can be a John the Baptist or a Steven in the Bible. I do know every chance I get, I will tell someone or anyone about my Jesus and how he holds me in the darkest nights. And that God loved me so much he sent his son so I can be with him one day at home in heaven. Because this world, this place, is not my home. I am as out of place here as a live pig at a barbecue.

The only reason I seem strong is the arms that hold me up. And when I'm tired and weak and ready to give up, he shows me his wonderful love and helps me to make it one more day. I love each of you no matter where I am.

Love,

Ruth Love

ABOUT THE AUTHOR

I was born in 1969. I grew up in a small town and in the country. I went to a small country church. I grew up and had 3 children by the time I was 21. I had 2 sisters and 1 brother whom I love. My mama and daddy was good people they teaches us to always help others. So growing up with same one always leaving with us showed us you always have to help others. My walk with God is same thing my mama and daddy always told us to do. To always give thanks to God for everything in our life.

These things happen to me and in the beginning I wrote it just for my grandkids no one else but as family and friends heard about it they told me I should get it published. When I finished writing the ones I told the most I heard God telling me to move forward with it I wasn't sure about it then out of the blue my cousin I had not heard from in about 25 yrs found me and we got to talking about my favorite thing God and I started telling her my God storys and she told me how they moved her and how I should write a book I told her I had one wrote and she told me that God would want me to share them with others to help people so I started looking and God lead me here. I live in Camden sc my life has not been easy but God has been there throw all of it. He is my rock.

Printed in the United States
By Bookmasters